Picture Reference

SPACE

SUE BECKLAKE

98-591

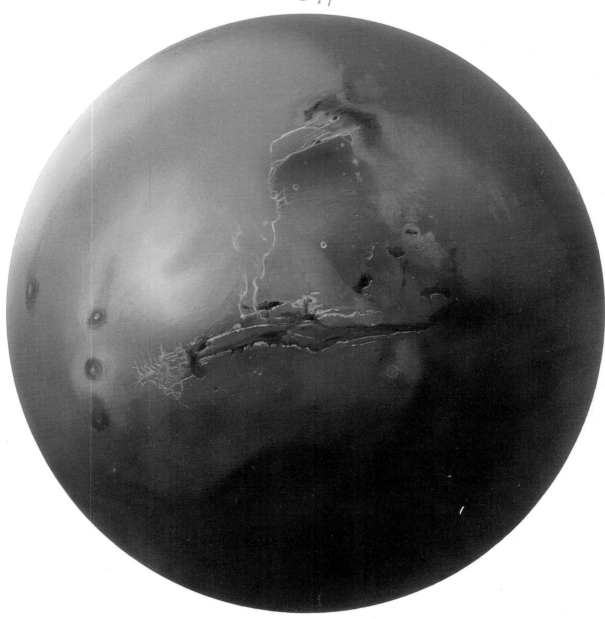

World Book

in association with

TWOCAN

How to use this book

Cross-references
Above the heading on the page, you will find a list of subjects that are related to the topic. These subjects are listed with their page numbers. Turn to these pages to find out more about each subject.

Glossary words
Difficult words are explained in the glossary on page 46. These words are written in **bold**. Look them up in the glossary to find out what they mean.

Index
The index is on pages 47–48. It is an alphabetical list of important words that are mentioned in the book. The page numbers on which these words occur are written next to them. If you want to read about a subject, look it up in the index, then turn to the page number given.

Titles in this series
Animals
Atlas
Space

First published in the United States and Canada by
World Book, Inc., 525 W. Monroe, Chicago, IL 60661
in association with Two-Can Publishing Ltd.

For information on World Book products, call 1-800-255-1750 x 2238, or visit us at our Web site at http://www.worldbook.com

Art director: Belinda Webster
Managing Editor: Deborah Kespert
Senior Designer: Helen Holmes
Editorial support: Samantha Hilton, Julia Hillyard
Consultant: Doug Millard, Associate Curator of Space Technology, Science Museum (UK)
Main Illustrations: Gary Bines (Blue Chip Illustration)
Computer illustrations: Mel Pickering
Special thanks to: Patricia Ohlenroth, World Book Publishing

Library of Congress Cataloging-in-Publication Data
Becklake, Sue.
  Space / Sue Becklake.
    p. cm. — (Picture reference)
  Includes index.
  Summary: Describes the solar system and its planets; discusses the science of studying space; includes "fact files," "amazing facts," and glossary.
  ISBN 0-7166-9900-1 (hbk.) — ISBN 0-7166-9901-X (pbk.)
  1. Outer space—Juvenile literature. 2. Solar system—Juvenile literature. 3. Astronautics in astronomy— Juvenile literature. [1. Outer space. 2. Solar system. 3. Astronautics. 4. Astronomy.]
  I. Title. II. Series: Picture reference (Chicago, Ill.)
  QB500.22.B44 1997   97-12168
  500.5—dc21

Photographic credits:
Ancient Art & Architecture Collection: p9tl; Genesis: p15l; Jet Propulsion Laboratory: p24tr, p25tr & bl, p29br, p30cl & tr, p33cr & bc; NASA: p12bl, p25tl, p35bl; Rex Features: p17tr; Robert Harding: p15tr; Science Photo Library/Martin Bond p26bl, SPL/Tony Hallas p43cr, SPL/NASA p21br & p31cr, SPL/Novosti Press Agency p31tr, SPL/David Nunuk p35tr, SPL/Roger Ressmeyer-Starlight p27br, SPL/Royal Greenwich Observatory p9br, SPL/Royal Observatory Edinburgh p34br & p42tr, SPL/John Sanford p35cr, SPL/Robin Scagell p10br; Tony Stone Images: p11t, p26bl; Zefa: p8cl.

Printed in Hong Kong

1 2 3 4 5 6 7 8 9 10 01 00 99 98 97

Contents

What is space?

Space is the near emptiness surrounding the Earth. It stretches farther than astronomers can see, even with their most powerful telescopes. In space, there are stars, **moons**, galaxies, and **planets,** including the Earth. Between the planets and stars, there are tiny bits of dust and **gas**. There may also be other things waiting to be discovered. Everything in space is part of the **universe**.

▶ Scientists think that the universe was formed about 10 to 15 **billion** years ago. These pictures show you what may have happened.

1 The universe probably began with a huge explosion that scientists call the Big Bang. Immediately after the Big Bang, the universe was small and very hot.

Big Bang

2 Then the universe cooled down and became larger. Huge swirls of dust and gas clung together to make galaxies.

Galaxy

Nebula

3 Inside the galaxies, there were smaller dust and gas clouds called nebulae. This is where the stars were born. One of these stars was the sun. It was born in a galaxy called the Milky Way.

Earth

Mercury

Sun

Venus

Solar system

Uranus

Mars

Jupiter

Saturn

Neptune

Pluto

4 Nine planets formed around the new sun to make the solar system. One of these planets was the Earth.

Go to Rocky planet page 30, Sun page 26

Earth

The Earth is a huge ball of rock traveling through space. It is one of nine **planets** that **orbit** the sun, and it formed about 4½ billion years ago. The Earth is different from the other planets because much of its surface is covered with water. It is also the only planet known to have life. It is home to many kinds of plants and animals. These things can live here because the Earth is just the right distance from the sun, making it neither too hot nor too cold.

▼ Below are the different layers that make up the Earth.

Crust
The crust is the top, rocky layer of the Earth. It makes up all the land and the ocean floor.

Mantle
Beneath the crust is a thick layer of hot rock called the mantle.

Outer core
Hot, melted iron forms the Earth's outer **core**.

.... Daytime

Earth   Sun

Nighttime

Day and night
The Earth spins around like a top. As it spins, only one side faces the sun. The side facing the sun has daytime and the side facing away has nighttime.

Life on Earth

Three to four **billion** years ago, early forms of life appeared in the ocean. They were too small to see, but they slowly developed into plants, jellyfish, and fish.

About 360 million years ago, some fish began to change and spend part of their time on land. Later, they began to live on land all the time.

Around 220 million years ago, enormous dinosaurs roamed the Earth. Suddenly, about 150 million years later, they were all wiped out.

Above the Earth

The air around the Earth forms its **atmosphere**. Air is made up of several **gases**, including **oxygen**. Below, you can see the different layers of the atmosphere. As you move away from the Earth, there is increasingly less air in the atmosphere until it disappears completely.

Into space...............
Space begins where there is no air left.

50-300 miles (80-480 km)
A space shuttle flies at 124 miles (200 km) above the Earth. There is hardly any air there.

30-50 miles (48-80 km)
Here, the air burns up tiny rocks from space to make meteors, or shooting stars.

Ozone layer
Some of the sun's rays can be harmful. A gas called ozone helps to stop these rays from reaching the Earth.

6-30 miles (10-48 km)
Some jet planes fly in this layer of the atmosphere above the clouds.

0-6 miles (0-10 km)
Close to the Earth, there is plenty of air. Most of the clouds are here.

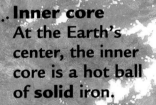

Inner core
At the Earth's center, the inner core is a hot ball of **solid** iron.

About 140 million years ago, the first birds appeared on the Earth. They had claws on their wings and probably developed from flying reptiles.

Humans have lived on Earth for about two million years. This is a short time compared with the dinosaurs. They lived on Earth about 80 times longer.

Factfile

It may reach 13,000 °F (7,000 °C) at the Earth's center. That's over 100 times hotter than the hottest desert.

The Earth measures 24,902 miles (40,075 kilometers) around its widest part. It would take 1½ years to walk all the way around.

*Sometimes hot rock from inside the Earth bursts out of the crust to form a **volcano**.*

Go to Galaxy page 42, Telescope page 10

Astronomer

Astronomers are people who study objects in space, such as the sun, moon, stars, and **planets**. They try to determine what these things are made of, where they are, and how fast they are traveling. Many objects in space are so far away that astronomers need to use powerful telescopes to study them properly. Astronomers are always searching the skies for new discoveries and trying to see farther into space than before.

Copernicus

Over 450 years ago, in 1543, a Polish astronomer called Copernicus suggested that all the planets, including the Earth, traveled around the sun. At the time, most other astronomers did not believe him. They could see the sun move across the sky, so they believed that the sun and the planets traveled around the Earth. Today, we know that these astronomers were wrong and that Copernicus's ideas were right.

The first astronomers

Long ago, the first astronomers used the movements of the sun, moon, stars, and planets to help people plan their daily lives. Astronomers built towers, such as the one above, to watch the sky. By looking at the different positions of objects in the sky, they could tell when the seasons were about to change and would estimate the best time for farmers to plant their seeds. They could also tell the time by watching the sun move across the sky during the day.

The wrong way

In Picture A, the sun and the planets travel around the Earth, so the Earth is at the center of the **universe**.

A

Earth

Sun

The right way

Picture B shows you how the planets really travel. Here the sun is at the center and the Earth and the other planets travel around it.

B

Sun

Earth

Galileo

Over 350 years ago, in 1610, an Italian astronomer named Galileo discovered that the planet Jupiter had four **moons** circling around it. This proved that everything did not travel around the Earth. It made people realize that Copernicus's ideas were right. In this picture you can see two of the telescopes Galileo used to make his discoveries.

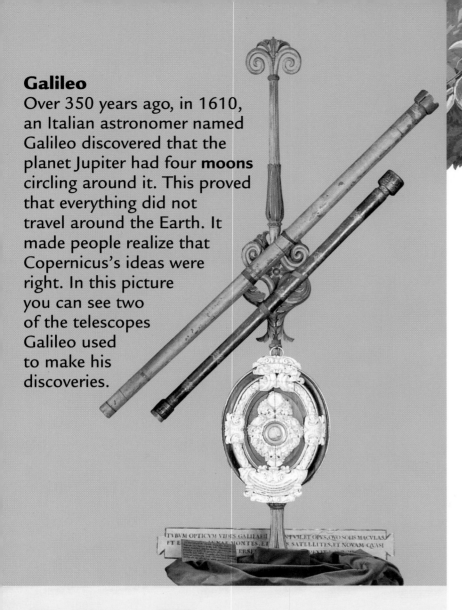

Newton

The English scientist Isaac Newton was born about 350 years ago in 1642. According to a story, he watched an apple drop from a tree and wondered why it fell straight to the ground. Then he realized that the Earth was pulling everything toward it. He called this **gravity**. Newton also determined why the planets traveled around the sun and did not shoot off in all directions into space. He realized that the sun's gravity pulled the planets and kept them in their paths around the sun.

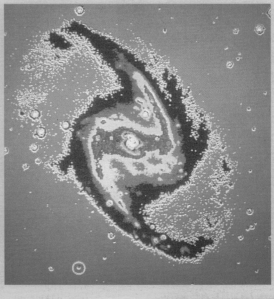

Modern astronomers

Today, many astronomers work in a control room with computers, such as the one below. They point a telescope at the sky and use it to make pictures of distant stars and galaxies. Computers then add colors to the pictures to make them clearer.

Adding color

A computer has added colors to this picture of a galaxy. The brightest parts are colored white.

Go to Astronomer page 8, Galaxy page 42, Space shuttle page 20

Telescope

A telescope is a tool that astronomers use to find out about space. It makes distant things, such as stars and **planets**, look bigger and nearer. Over 350 years ago, an Italian astronomer named Galileo became the first person to study the night sky with a telescope. Today, telescopes are more powerful than Galileo's and astronomers can see much farther into space.

Tube
Light from stars and planets enters the telescope tube.

Eyepiece
An astronomer looks through the eyepiece.

Simple telescope
People who study the stars at home often look through a simple telescope, such as the one on the left. Sometimes a camera is fitted to the telescope. It can take photographs that show more detail than the eye can see.

Light

Eyepiece

Mirror

How a telescope works
A curved mirror inside the tube collects light from stars and planets and makes a picture, or image, of part of the sky. An eyepiece makes this image look bigger.

Stand
A stand keeps the telescope steady.

Observatory
Large modern telescopes are often built on mountaintops where the sky is clear. Several telescopes are usually grouped together at a place called an observatory. Each telescope is inside a dome-shaped building. A slit in the dome opens to let the telescope point at the sky and take photographs that an astronomer can study. The dome turns around so that the telescope can point at any part of the sky.

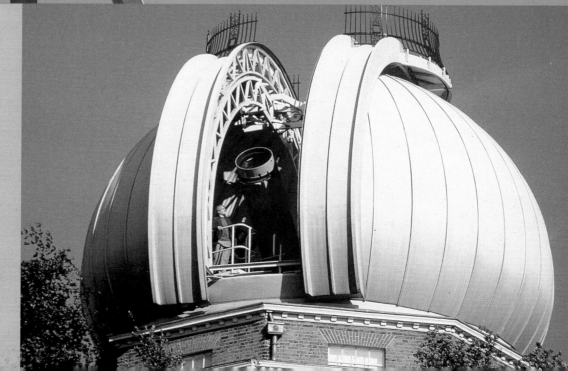

Radio telescope

Many objects in space, such as distant galaxies, give out **radio waves**. Astronomers collect these waves with radio telescopes, which look like large dishes. A group of telescopes works together, using the radio waves to make a picture of the object in space. The radio telescopes in this photograph are part of the Very Large Array Telescope in New Mexico, which has 27 dishes linked together.

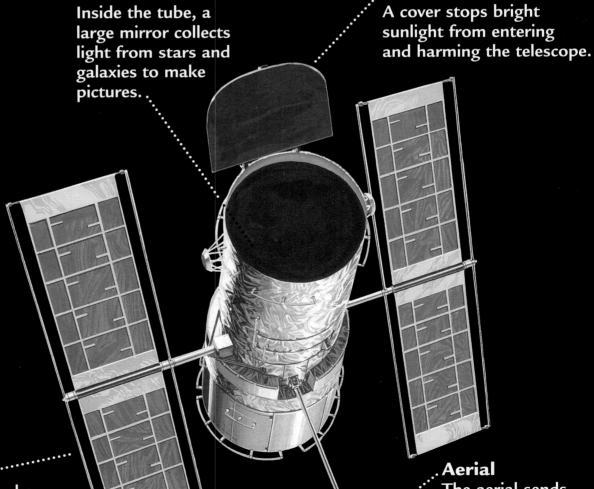

Hubble Space Telescope

There is a telescope in space that circles around the Earth. It is named after the astronomer Edwin Hubble, and it was **launched** in 1990 by the space shuttle. Hubble can see farther than larger telescopes on the Earth. This is because in space there are no clouds, dust, or moving air to blur its view. Hubble has taken photographs of many distant stars and galaxies.

Mirror
Inside the tube, a large mirror collects light from stars and galaxies to make pictures.

Cover
A cover stops bright sunlight from entering and harming the telescope.

Solar panel
The solar panels make **electricity** from sunlight to keep the telescope working.

Aerial
The aerial sends down radio-wave messages to Earth.

Go to Astronaut page 16, Rocket page 14, Solar system page 28, Sun page 26

Moon

The moon is a ball of rock that circles around the Earth about once every 27 days. The same side of the moon, called the nearside, always faces the Earth. The other side, called the farside, is hidden from the Earth. The moon is the only place in space that astronauts have visited. Twelve astronauts have landed there to explore its surface and bring back rocks. They discovered that the moon was dry and dusty and that nothing lived there.

Surface
The moon's surface is covered with thousands of **craters**. They were made millions of years ago, when rocks from space crashed into the moon.

Crater
A crater has a ring of mountains around its edges. Sometimes there are also mountains in the middle of a crater.

Mountain
Long lines of mountains run across some parts of the moon. These mountains are called the Apennines.

Streak
These streaks on the moon's surface were made when melted rock was flung out of a newly formed crater.

Moon walking
This astronaut is collecting rocks. He has to wear a spacesuit to breathe because there is no air on the moon. His footprints will remain there for thousands of years because there is neither wind nor rain to erase them.

Moon

Earth

Sun

Moonlight
The moon looks bright at night, but it does not make its own light. Instead, the sun shines on the moon, lighting up one side. On moonlit nights, people are really seeing sunlight that has bounced off the moon and down toward the Earth.

Factfile

In the sunlight, the moon is twice as hot as the hottest desert on Earth, but in the dark, it is twice as cold as the coldest place on Earth.

In 1959, a Russian **spacecraft** *called Luna 3 sent the first pictures of the farside of the moon back to Earth.*

The moon is bigger than the smallest **planet**, *which is Pluto.*

Sea
Each large dark patch on the moon is called a sea. But there is no water on the moon, so the seas are dry.

Full moon   **Crescent moon**

Moon shapes
As the moon travels around the Earth, you can see different amounts of the side lit by the sun. Sometimes, the moon looks round. This is called a full moon. At other times, it may have a crescent shape.

Tides
Twice a day on the Earth, oceans rise up the shore and fall back down again. This is caused by the moon's **gravity** pulling the oceans toward the moon.

Go to Astronaut page 16, Moon page 12, Satellite page 22

Rocket

A rocket is a **vehicle** that can carry astronauts or satellites into space. It has powerful **engines** that burn **fuel**, pushing it up into the sky. Most rockets have two or three sections, called stages. Each stage has its own engines and fuel. The stages burn up their fuel one at a time and then drop away. This makes the rocket lighter, letting it travel faster and faster until it reaches space.

Escape rocket
An escape rocket could carry the astronauts away if something went wrong.

Apollo spacecraft
The astronauts traveled to the moon inside the Apollo **spacecraft**.

Third stage
The third stage provided extra power to send the astronauts to the moon.

Saturn V
Saturn V was one of the most powerful types of rockets ever built. Between 1969 and 1972, it was used for the Apollo missions to take astronauts to land on the moon. Five main engines lifted the rocket off the **launch pad** until it was traveling 70 times faster than a car on a highway.

Second stage
The second stage was smaller than the first stage. It lifted the astronauts into space.

UNITED STATES

First stage
Inside the first stage, there were two large tanks that held the fuel for the five main engines.

USA   USA

Engine
The five main engines were at the bottom of the rocket.

Crawler
This crawler carried the rocket to the launch pad. It moved so slowly that a person could walk to the launch pad faster than it could crawl there.

14

To the moon and back

During an Apollo mission, three astronauts traveled to the moon in the small Apollo spacecraft, but only two of them landed. One astronaut stayed in the spacecraft, circling the moon, while the other two flew down to the surface in the **lunar lander**. The astronauts came back to Earth in the part of the spacecraft shown on the right. They landed in the sea and were picked up by a ship waiting nearby.

7 The satellite at the top of the third stage is carried higher. It is then released into **orbit** around the Earth.

6 The second stage drops away, leaving only the third stage and the satellite.

5 The covers that protect the satellite are thrown off.

4 The second stage engines start firing to push the rest of the rocket up.

3 When the first stage has used up its fuel, it drops away as well.

2 The **booster rockets** soon use up their fuel and fall away into the sea.

1 The Ariane rocket blasts off, carrying its satellite into space.

Ariane

Ariane is a type of rocket that launches satellites. Astronauts do not travel on board. The rocket is controlled from Earth by scientists.

Astronaut

Astronauts are men and women who travel in
space to explore such places as the moon or to
carry out experiments. They also repair **machines**,
such as telescopes and satellites. There is no air in
space, so when astronauts leave their **spacecraft,**
they must wear **spacesuits** that provide them with
air to breathe. Astronauts have to train for a long
time before they are ready to travel into space.

Astronaut training

Floating
in a water
tank helps
teach an
astronaut
how it
feels to be
weightless.

In space, there is no
right way up.
A spinning
chair helps
an astronaut
imagine
how this
feels.

An
astronaut
learns how
to fly a
spacecraft
by studying
its flight
controls.

Cooling tube
It can become hot inside
a spacesuit, so tubes
pump cool water around
the suit to cool down
the astronaut.

Pocket
An astronaut's
spacesuit has
pockets on it that
hold small tools.

Astronaut's glove
These special gloves screw
on the spacesuit. They let
the astronaut's fingers
bend to do work.

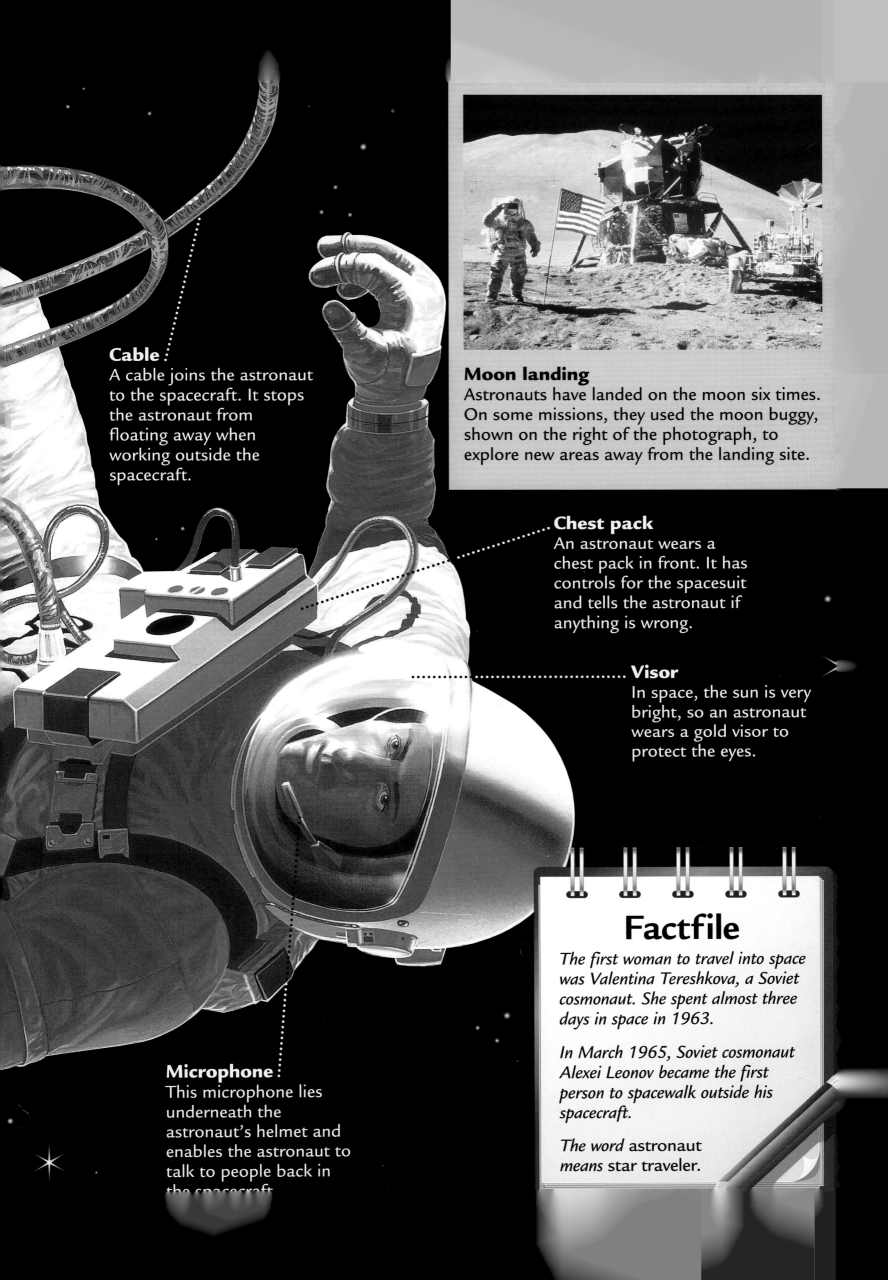

Cable
A cable joins the astronaut to the spacecraft. It stops the astronaut from floating away when working outside the spacecraft.

Moon landing
Astronauts have landed on the moon six times. On some missions, they used the moon buggy, shown on the right of the photograph, to explore new areas away from the landing site.

Chest pack
An astronaut wears a chest pack in front. It has controls for the spacesuit and tells the astronaut if anything is wrong.

Visor
In space, the sun is very bright, so an astronaut wears a gold visor to protect the eyes.

Microphone
This microphone lies underneath the astronaut's helmet and enables the astronaut to talk to people back in the spacecraft.

Factfile

The first woman to travel into space was Valentina Tereshkova, a Soviet cosmonaut. She spent almost three days in space in 1963.

In March 1965, Soviet cosmonaut Alexei Leonov became the first person to spacewalk outside his spacecraft.

The word astronaut *means* star traveler.

Space station

A space station is a home in space. Astronauts live here and carry out experiments to learn more about how space affects people. Inside the space station, there is air to breathe, so the astronauts do not need to wear spacesuits. In 1986, Russia **launched** a new space station called Mir. Rockets brought up the station's different parts and joined them together in space.

▶ **Mir space station**

Control desk
Astronauts control the space station from here.

Solar panel
These panels use the sun's rays to make **electricity**, which provides power for the space station.

Living quarters
Astronauts sleep, eat, and work in the living quarters. This was the first part of Mir to be launched into space.

Factfile

There have been nine space stations, including Skylab, Salyut, and Mir, but Mir is the only one still in space.

In 1988, on board the Mir space station, Musa Manarov and Vladimir Titov became the first astronauts to live in space for over one year.

There are plans to build a new space station, called Alpha, by 2010.

Astronauts stand in a big bag to take a shower. A tube sucks away the water when they have finished washing.

Astronauts must drink through straws to stop any liquids from floating away. They eat food that comes in closed foil packets.

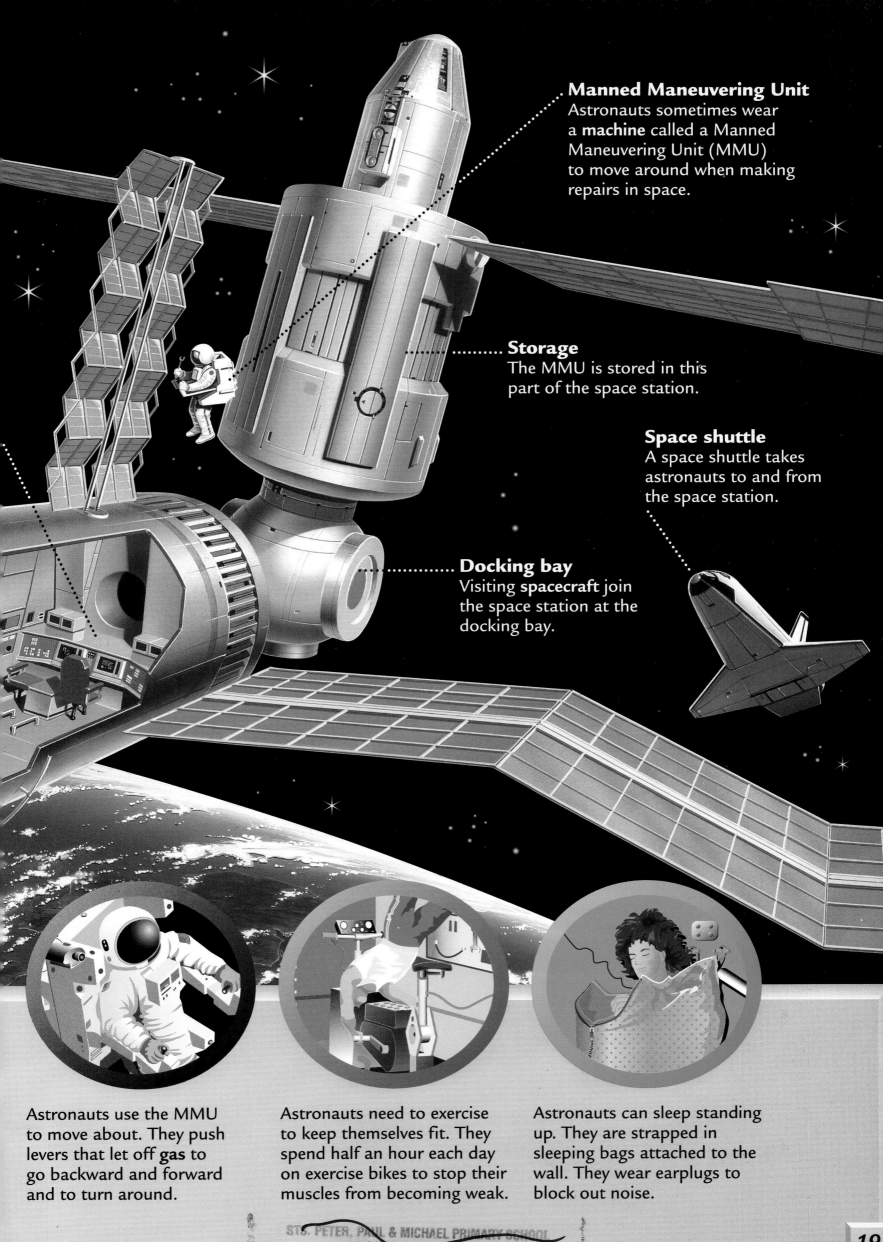

Manned Maneuvering Unit
Astronauts sometimes wear a **machine** called a Manned Maneuvering Unit (MMU) to move around when making repairs in space.

Storage
The MMU is stored in this part of the space station.

Space shuttle
A space shuttle takes astronauts to and from the space station.

Docking bay
Visiting **spacecraft** join the space station at the docking bay.

Astronauts use the MMU to move about. They push levers that let off **gas** to go backward and forward and to turn around.

Astronauts need to exercise to keep themselves fit. They spend half an hour each day on exercise bikes to stop their muscles from becoming weak.

Astronauts can sleep standing up. They are strapped in sleeping bags attached to the wall. They wear earplugs to block out noise.

Go to Astronaut page 16, Satellite page 22, Space probe page 24, Space station page 18, Telescope page 10

Space shuttle

A space shuttle is a special plane that can fly into space and back to Earth many times. It can take astronauts to a space station or launch a satellite or space probe. A shuttle has several parts. The part that carries the astronauts is called the shuttle orbiter. The other parts are a huge **fuel** tank and two **booster rockets**. The fuel tank is the only part of the space shuttle that cannot be used again.

Space shuttle orbiter

Cargo bay
Cameras and telescopes in the cargo bay take pictures of the Earth or study the stars in space.

Take off and landing

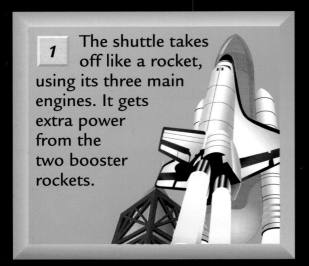

1 The shuttle takes off like a rocket, using its three main engines. It gets extra power from the two booster rockets.

Tile
When the shuttle comes back to Earth, it becomes very hot. Thousands of special tiles stop it from burning up.

2 When the fuel from the boosters is used up, they fall into the sea. The large fuel tank will fall away too.

Engine
The three main engines are not used in space. Smaller engines move the shuttle and take it back toward the Earth.

3 The shuttle orbiter lands with its engines switched off. It glides down to the runway on Earth like an airplane.

Cargo bay door
In space, the doors of the cargo bay are open to let extra heat from the cabin escape.

Spacelab
Spacelab is a **laboratory** where the astronauts work. The shuttle carries the lab within its cargo bay.

Robot arm
The robot arm can launch or capture a satellite. Astronauts can attach themselves to the arm to make repairs to the satellite.

Cabin
On the upper deck of the cabin, there are controls for flying the shuttle. The astronauts eat, sleep, and work on a deck below.

Tunnel
An astronaut floats through a tunnel to move from the shuttle cabin to Spacelab.

Factfile

There are four shuttle orbiters. They are called Columbia, Atlantis, Discovery, and Endeavour.

On January 28, 1986, the shuttle Challenger exploded 73 seconds after takeoff, killing all seven astronauts on board.

During takeoff, the power of a shuttle's engines is the same as 140 jumbo jets.

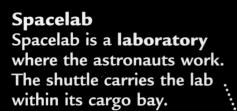

Into space
In April 1990, the Hubble Space Telescope was launched by the space shuttle Discovery. An astronaut in the shuttle cabin worked the controls for the robot arm, which put the telescope into **orbit**.

Satellite

A satellite is a **machine** that circles around the Earth. There are many kinds of satellites, and they do different jobs. Some study the weather or the Earth's surface, and others send messages from one part of the world to another. Satellites have different **orbits** depending on the job they do. Powerful rockets carry the satellites up into space and put them into the right orbit.

▶ These are four of the satellites **orbiting** around the Earth.

Navstar
A satellite, such as Navstar, helps ships and planes find their way, or navigate.

Meteosat
Meteosat is a weather satellite. It monitors the clouds and measures the strength of the wind. It also sends to Earth information on the **temperature** of the land, sea, and air.

A television forecaster uses the measurements from a weather satellite to tell people what the weather will be like over several days.

Messages sent by Navstar tell a captain where his ship is, even in bad weather. They can also tell him how fast the ship is traveling.

Satellite pictures from Landsat are studied by scientists. They can show how well crops are growing, spot forest fires, and be used to make maps of the Earth.

22

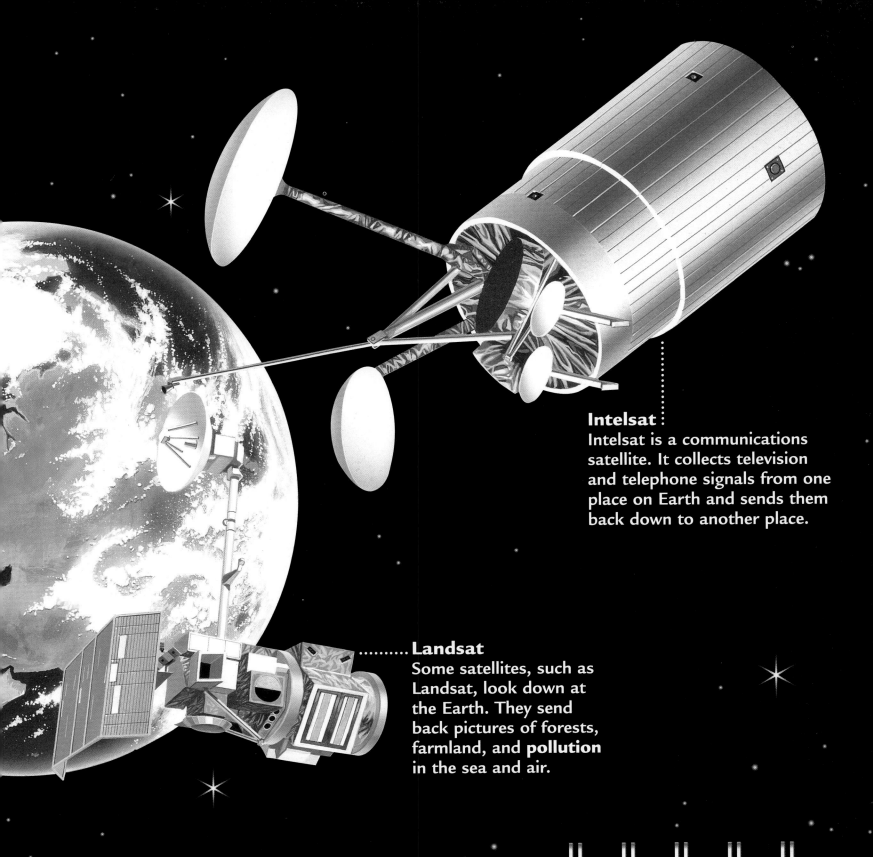

Intelsat
Intelsat is a communications satellite. It collects television and telephone signals from one place on Earth and sends them back down to another place.

Landsat
Some satellites, such as Landsat, look down at the Earth. They send back pictures of forests, farmland, and **pollution** in the sea and air.

A telephone conversation may travel up to a communications satellite and then down to someone on the end of a phone in another country.

A communications satellite sends television programs from one country to another, so people all over the world can watch them.

Factfile

In 1957, Russia launched Sputnik 1, which was the world's first satellite. It circled the Earth in just over 1½ hours.

Today, there are more than 450 working satellites circling the Earth.

The first weather satellite to send pictures of clouds back to Earth was called Tiros. It was launched in April 1960.

Go to Comet and asteroid page 34, Gas planet page 32, Rocky planet page 30

Space probe

A space probe is a **machine** that explores space and sends information and pictures back to the Earth. Astronauts do not travel in a space probe. Instead, it is controlled by scientists on the ground. Some probes are launched by a rocket, others by a space shuttle. Probes have visited many **moons** and all the **planets** except Pluto. They have sent back information about the weather, **temperature**, and surface of these places.

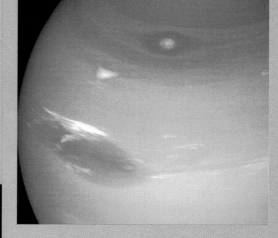

Dark spot
In 1989, a space probe found a dark spot on the planet Neptune. It was a huge storm about the size of Earth, but it now seems to have disappeared.

Neptune

Uranus

Voyager 2 space probe

Saturn

Jupiter

Voyager
In 1977, two space probes called Voyager 1 and 2 set out to visit the giant planets farthest away from the sun. Both probes flew past Jupiter and Saturn, and Voyager 2 also went on to visit Uranus and Neptune. Its journey from the Earth to Neptune took 12 years. The probes sent back close-up pictures of the planets' cloudy surfaces and discovered many new moons.

Viking

In 1976, two probes named Viking reached the planet Mars. The probes circled around Mars, making maps of its surface, while **landers** traveled to the ground. These landers tested rocks and soil to see if anything lived there, but they found nothing. You can see a Viking lander below. In 1996, more probes were sent to explore other parts of Mars.

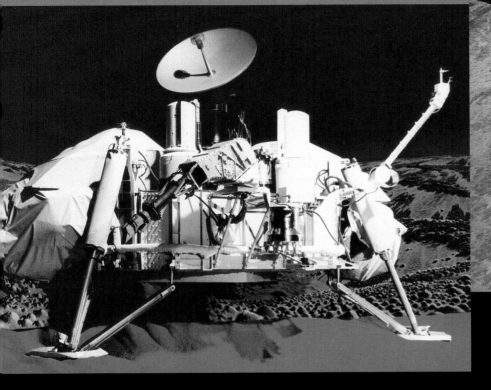

Magellan

The Magellan space probe arrived at Venus in 1990. It could not take photographs because thick clouds hid the planet's surface. Instead, it bounced **radio waves** off the planet. Computers on the Earth were then able to make pictures from these radio waves. This picture shows mountains and **volcanoes** on Venus's surface. The dark parts are the places that Magellan missed.

Galileo

The most recent probe to visit Jupiter is called Galileo. It arrived in 1995, after a six-year journey. The main probe dropped a smaller probe, shown on the right, by parachute into Jupiter's clouds. For nearly an hour, it sent information about the clouds up to the main probe and then back to scientists waiting on the Earth. The main probe then circled around Jupiter and visited its four large moons.

Jupiter

small probe

Ida

The Galileo space probe sent back the first ever close-up photographs of space rocks, or asteroids. It saw this one, called Ida, on its way to Jupiter.

Go to Earth page 6, Moon page 12, Solar system page 28, Star page 36

Sun

The sun is a huge fiery ball of **gas** that glows in the sky. It is the closest star to the Earth. Like all stars, the sun gives out **energy** as heat and light. Much of this is lost in space but some of it reaches the Earth. Without heat and light, the Earth would be dark and cold and nothing could live here.

Warming the Earth
The sun always warms the Earth, but it shines more strongly on some places than on others. At the far north and south of the Earth, the sun shines weakly, so the land is always cold. At the middle of the Earth, the sun shines strongly. There, it is always warm.

Using sunlight
The panels on the roof of this house use sunlight to make **electricity**, which runs such **machines** as a stove and a television.

Flare
Sometimes hot gas bursts out of the sun as a flare.

Prominence
A prominence is a huge tongue or loop of gas that rises high above the sun's surface.

WARNING!
Never look directly at the sun. Its light is so bright that it could harm your eyes.

Corona
The corona is the name of the layer of thin gas all around the sun.

Sun's surface
Hot gas bubbles up on the sun's surface and glows yellow.

Core
The **core** is where the sun makes its energy.

Factfile

Light from the sun travels almost 93 million miles (150 million km) to reach the Earth. It would take a car over 200 years to travel this far, but it takes light only eight minutes.

In ancient times, many Chinese people believed that an eclipse was a dragon eating the sun.

The sun spins around once every 27 days.

Under the sun's surface
Here, churning gas carries energy to the surface of the sun where it can escape.

Sunspot
Dark patches on the sun are called sunspots. These areas are cooler than the rest of the sun's surface.

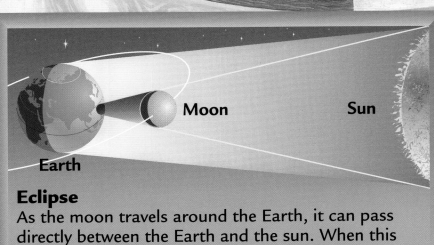

Moon

Sun

Earth

Eclipse
As the moon travels around the Earth, it can pass directly between the Earth and the sun. When this happens, the sun is completely hidden for a few minutes. This is an eclipse of the sun.

Ring of light
During an eclipse of the sun, the moon blocks out most of the sun's light. Only the pale glow of the sun's corona can be seen.

Go to Gas planet page 32, Moon page 12, Rocky planet page 30, Sun page 26

Solar system

The solar system is the name given to the sun and all the objects in space that travel around it. In the solar system, there are nine **planets** and their **moons**, comets, and chunks of rock called asteroids and meteoroids. The planets lie huge distances apart and take different lengths of time to travel around the sun. The time it takes for a planet to circle the sun once is called its year. The planets also spin around like tops. The time it takes for a planet to spin around once is its day.

▼ The planets are the largest objects in the solar system except for the sun.

Jupiter
Jupiter is larger than all the other planets put together.

Mars
Mars is about half the size of the Earth and much colder.

Moon

Earth
Earth is the third planet from the sun. Many different plants and animals live here.

Venus
Venus is the nearest planet to the Earth, and almost the same size.

Mercury
The only planet smaller than Mercury is Pluto.

sun

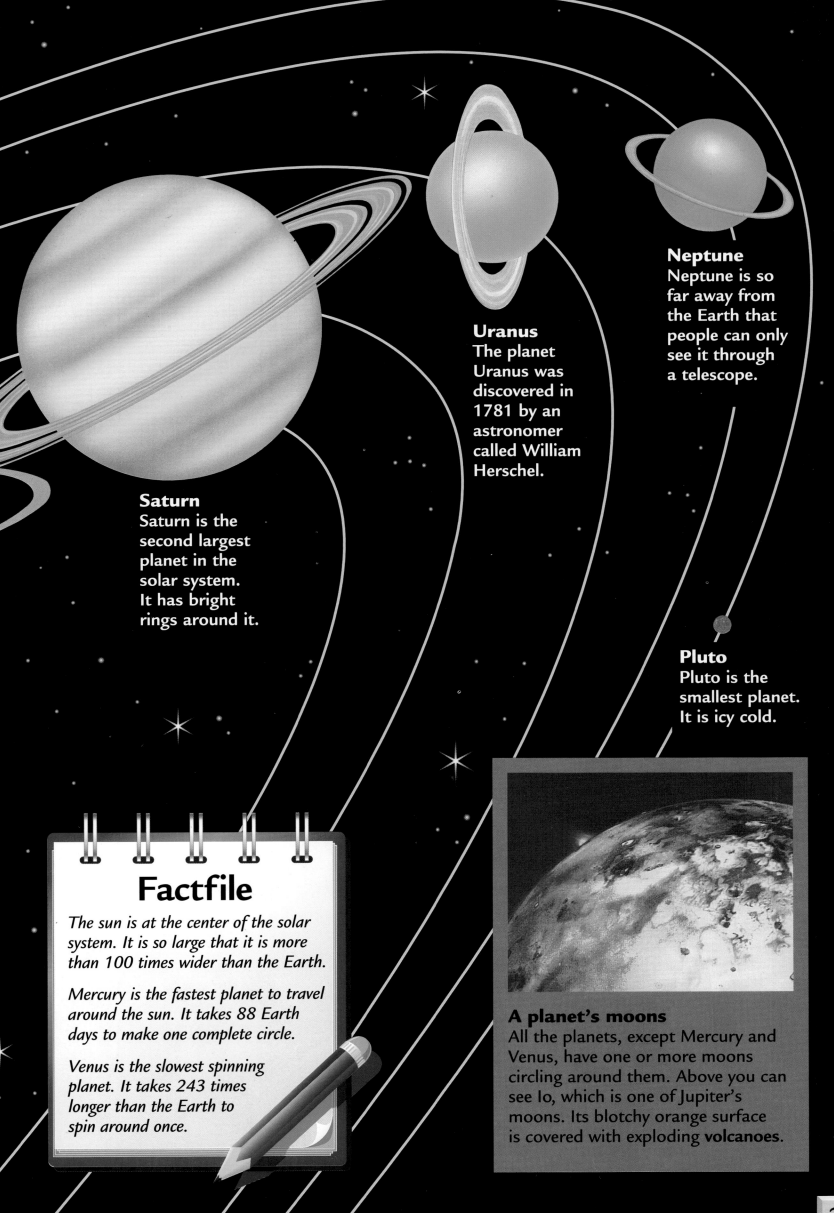

Neptune
Neptune is so far away from the Earth that people can only see it through a telescope.

Uranus
The planet Uranus was discovered in 1781 by an astronomer called William Herschel.

Saturn
Saturn is the second largest planet in the solar system. It has bright rings around it.

Pluto
Pluto is the smallest planet. It is icy cold.

Factfile

The sun is at the center of the solar system. It is so large that it is more than 100 times wider than the Earth.

Mercury is the fastest planet to travel around the sun. It takes 88 Earth days to make one complete circle.

Venus is the slowest spinning planet. It takes 243 times longer than the Earth to spin around once.

A planet's moons
All the planets, except Mercury and Venus, have one or more moons circling around them. Above you can see Io, which is one of Jupiter's moons. Its blotchy orange surface is covered with exploding **volcanoes**.

Go to Earth page 6, Solar system page 28, Space probe page 24

Rocky planet

A rocky **planet** is made up of rock and metal. It has a rocky surface with a metal **core**. The four planets nearest the sun, which are Mercury, Venus, Earth, and Mars, are all rocky planets. Pluto, the planet farthest away from the sun, is similar to them, but its core is made of rock instead of metal. Pluto is so cold that its surface is covered with a thick layer of ice.

Crashing into Venus
This crater was made by a rock that hit Venus. All the rocky planets in the solar system have craters on their surface.

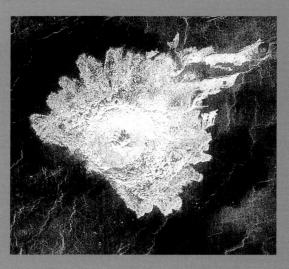

Venus
Venus is nearly the same size as the Earth but it would not be a good planet for astronauts to visit because it is covered with thick, poisonous clouds. These clouds keep Venus even hotter than Mercury, although it is farther away from the sun. The air on Venus presses down so hard that space probes have been crushed when they landed there.

Crust
The outer layer, or crust, of Venus is made of rock.

Mercury
Mercury looks similar to the moon. It is covered with thousands of **craters** that formed when rocks from space crashed into it millions of years ago. The side of Mercury that faces the sun is over seven times hotter than the hottest desert on Earth. The side facing away from the sun is extremely cold. There is no air or water on Mercury.

Surface
Venus has mountains, craters, and **volcanoes** on its surface.

Core
The core of Venus is made of a metal called iron.

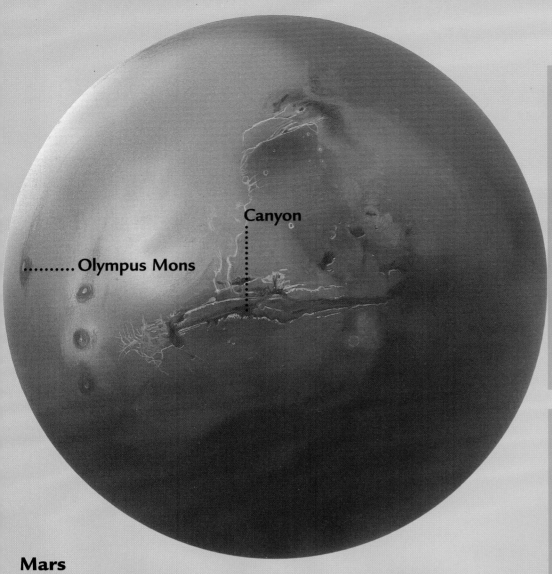

Canyon

.... Olympus Mons

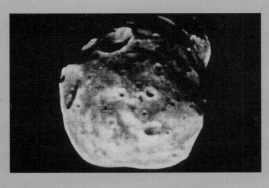

Two moons
Mars has two small rocky **moons**, that are shaped like potatoes and covered with craters. This is the larger moon called Phobos. The smaller moon is called Deimos.

On the surface
Rust-colored sand and rocks lie on the surface of Mars.

Mars
Mars is a dry and dusty planet. Its winds whip up huge dust storms that make its sky look pink. Large deserts, deep **canyons,** and giant volcanoes cover Mars. The biggest volcano in the solar system is there. Its name is Olympus Mons. Mars is called the red planet because from the Earth it looks red in the sky.

Pluto
Pluto is a tiny planet right at the edge of the solar system. It is so small and far away that astronomers do not know much about it. Pluto was discovered in 1930. Then, in 1978, astronomers found that it had a moon, which they named Charon. This is how Pluto and Charon might look from a visiting spacecraft.

Charon

Pluto

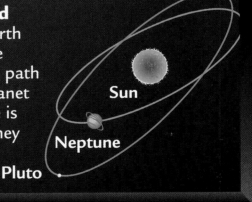

Traveling around
Pluto takes 248 Earth years to travel once around the sun. Its path crosses with the planet Neptune, but there is little danger that they will hit each other.

Sun

Neptune

Pluto

Planet X
A few astronomers think there may be another planet, which they call Planet X, that may be even farther away from us than Pluto. They are watching space probes speeding out of the solar system to see if they can find this new planet. These probes have now passed Pluto, but there has been no sign of Planet X yet.

Go to Astronomer page 8, Solar system page 28, Space probe page 24

Gas planet

A gas **planet** is made up mostly of **gases** and **liquids**. It has a rocky **core** that is covered in a thick layer of liquid or ice. On the outside of a gas planet, there are layers of colored clouds. Jupiter, Saturn, Uranus, and Neptune are gas planets. If astronauts ever manage to visit these distant places, they would not be able to explore them on foot, because there is no hard surface on which a **spacecraft** could land.

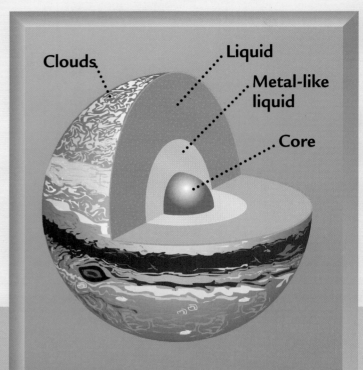

Clouds · Liquid · Metal-like liquid · Core

Inside Jupiter
Jupiter is made up of four different layers. At the center, there is a small, rocky core. Then, there are two layers of liquid. Jupiter's surface is made up of red and yellow swirling clouds.

Jupiter
The biggest planet in the solar system is Jupiter. Measuring across the middle, it is more than 11 times larger than the Earth. Jupiter spins faster than any other planet too. It is also very bright, which makes it easy to spot in the night sky. Venus is the only planet in the solar system that is brighter.

All the gas planets have rings around them. Jupiter's ring is so thin that it is difficult to see.

..The red and white spots in Jupiter's clouds are storms. The largest of these storms is called the Great Red Spot. It is bigger than planet Earth and has lasted for at least 300 years.

Titan

Saturn

Saturn

Saturn is the lightest planet in the solar system, and if it were placed on an enormous sea it would float. It also spins around so fast that it bulges out in the middle. More **moons orbit** Saturn than any other planet. Astronomers have counted 18 so far. Some of Saturn's moons are shown on the right.

Mimas

Tethys

Dione

Enceladus

Saturn's rings

Saturn has the brightest and widest rings of any of the gas planets. They are thin and flat and made up of pieces of ice. These pieces can be tiny flakes or chunks as large as a house.

Uranus

Uranus is covered by green and blue clouds. It lies almost completely on its side as it orbits the sun, rolling around like a marble. It has 15 moons and 9 thin, dark rings.

Neptune

Neptune's surface has a layer of bright blue clouds with wispy white clouds lying above. Most of the gas planets are stormy, but the winds that blow on Neptune are the fastest of all. Eight moons orbit Neptune. Six of these moons were discovered by the Voyager 2 space probe.

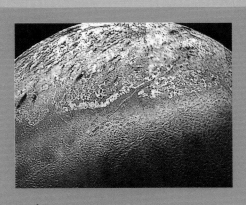

Triton

Triton is Neptune's largest moon and the coldest known place in the solar system.

to Earth page 6, Solar system page 28, Space probe page 24, Telescope page 10

Comet and asteroid

Comets and asteroids are part of the solar system. Like **planets** and **moons**, they travel around the sun. Comets are made of dust and ice and look like dirty snowballs. Astronomers think there are millions of them traveling through space. Asteroids are chunks of rock. The biggest asteroids are hundreds of miles wide but most are as small as pebbles.

A comet's path
A comet travels from the edge of the solar system toward the sun. It then swings around the sun and heads away again.

A comet's tail
A comet is too small to see from the Earth, except when it comes close to the sun. Then the sun's heat melts some of the comet's ice, making a huge cloud of dust and **gas**. This streams into a long tail, which is sometimes bright enough to see in the night sky. The tail of the comet points away from the sun.

Head
The icy center of a comet is hidden inside its head, under a glowing dust cloud.

Tail
A comet's tail can be 100 million miles (160 million kilometers) long.

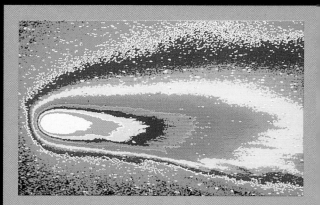

Halley's comet
Halley's comet comes close to the sun once about every 76 years. This **false-color** photograph was taken when it last appeared in 1986.

Meteor

As the Earth travels through space, it bumps into small rocks and dust left behind from comets. When the rocks and dust hit the top of the Earth's **atmosphere,** they burn up, making bright trails in the sky. Astronomers call these trails meteors, or shooting stars. Sometimes, the rocks are too large to burn up. They fall to the ground and are called meteorites.

In the sky
A meteor can look like a bright streak in the sky. It lasts for only a few seconds and then disappears.

Crashing to Earth
About 50 thousand years ago, a large meteorite crashed into the desert in Arizona and made this **crater.**

Asteroid

Astronomers have counted several thousands of asteroids but think there are millions more. Most are too small to be seen from the Earth, even with a telescope. The asteroid below is called Gaspra. Its photograph was taken by the Galileo space probe, as it flew past on its way to the planet Jupiter.

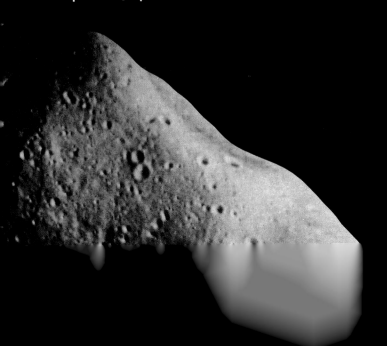

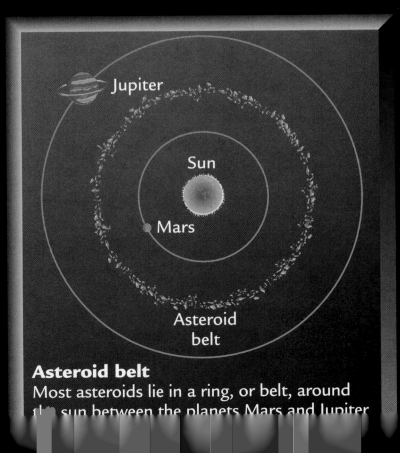

Jupiter

Sun

Mars

Asteroid belt

Asteroid belt
Most asteroids lie in a ring, or belt, around the sun between the planets Mars and Jupiter.

Go to Galaxy page 42, Sun page 26, Telescope page 10

Star

A star is a huge fiery ball of **gas** that gives out heat and light. The sun is a star and the only one to look like a huge ball in the sky. All the other stars look like pinpoints of light because they are so far away. Stars are not all the same. They are different colors and sizes. Each star also has a lifetime. Once it is born, it will shine steadily for a long time, until it dies.

▶ During its life, a star changes several times. At each stage it looks different.

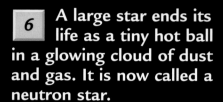

6 A large star ends its life as a tiny hot ball in a glowing cloud of dust and gas. It is now called a neutron star.

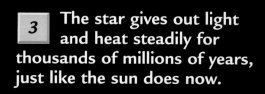

1 A star begins its life inside a large cloud of dust and gas called a nebula.

2 A clump of gas inside the nebula shrinks into a ball, which becomes hotter and starts to glow. This ball is a new star.

Factfile

On a clear night, you can see over a thousand stars in the sky without using a telescope.

The hottest star that astronomers have found is nearly 40 times hotter than the sun.

*In about five **billion** years, the sun will swell up to a giant star. It may become large enough to swallow up the Earth.*

3 The star gives out light and heat steadily for thousands of millions of years, just like the sun does now.

The stars in the sky look like single stars, but many of them are really two stars. Pairs of stars often circle around one another. These kinds of stars are called double stars.

A large group of stars is called a cluster. Most new stars, such as these shown in the picture, are in open clusters, while old stars are often tightly packed in round clusters.

5 A very large star may then explode, throwing out gas and dust in all directions. This explosion is called a supernova.

The sun seems to be the largest star in the sky, but it is really a medium-sized star and it is not particularly bright. The sun only seems larger because it is closer to the Earth than the other stars.

Some stars are hotter than others. The color of a star shows how hot it is. The hottest stars are white and the coolest are red. In-between are such yellow stars as the sun.

When a large star dies, it may fall in on itself, or collapse, sucking in everything nearby. It even traps light. This is called a black hole. Nothing can escape from a black hole.

4 Toward the end of its life, a star swells up into a huge red ball known as a red giant.

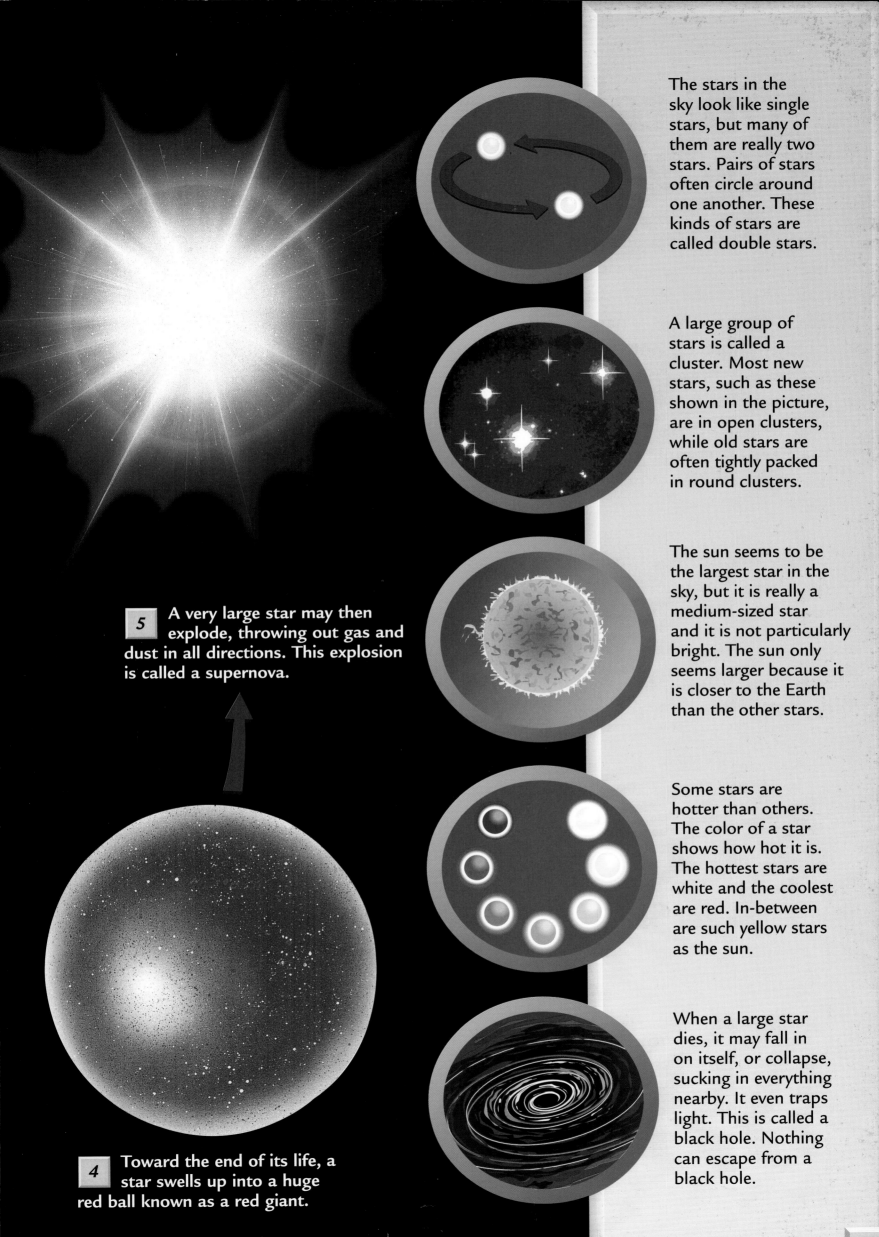

Go to Constellations of the southern skies page 40, Star page 36

Constellations
of the northern skies

A constellation is a group of stars that makes a pattern in the sky. Astronomers have counted 88 constellations and given each of them a name. The constellations do not change their shape, but as the night passes, they seem to move across the sky. This happens because the Earth is spinning around. The constellations themselves are not really moving. People see different constellations depending on where they live in the world.

▶ This picture shows the main constellations you can see in the northern half of the world. The United States and Canada are in this part of the world.

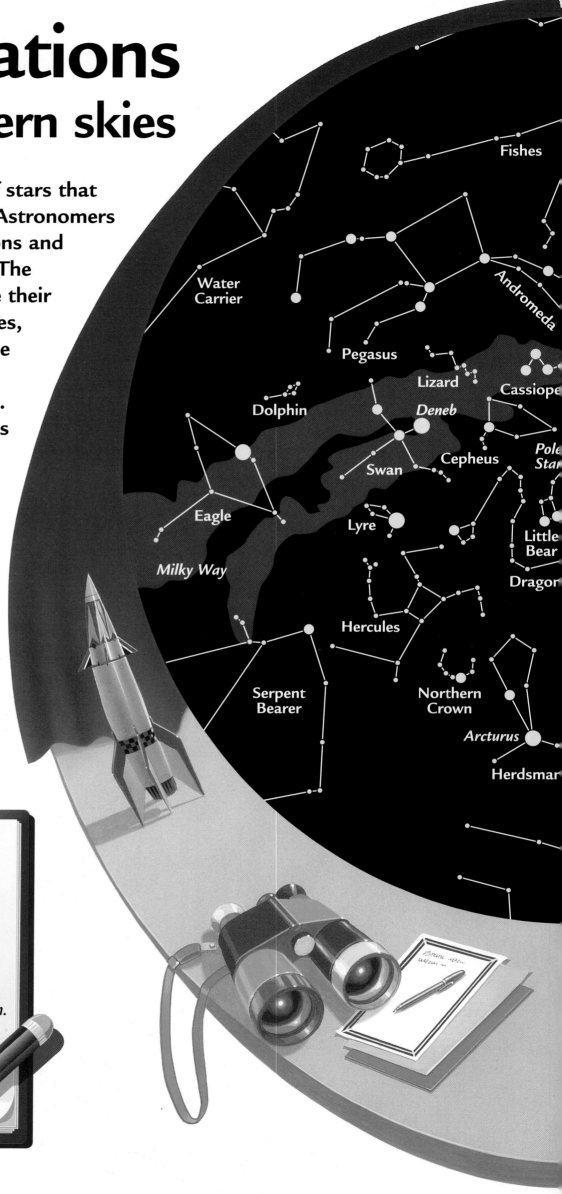

Factfile

The brightest star you can see in the northern sky is called Arcturus. It is part of the Herdsman constellation.

The constellations seem to twinkle in the sky. This happens because moving air blurs starlight as it travels to Earth.

The faint Lynx constellation took its name from an animal with sharp eyesight, because you need sharp eyesight to spot it.

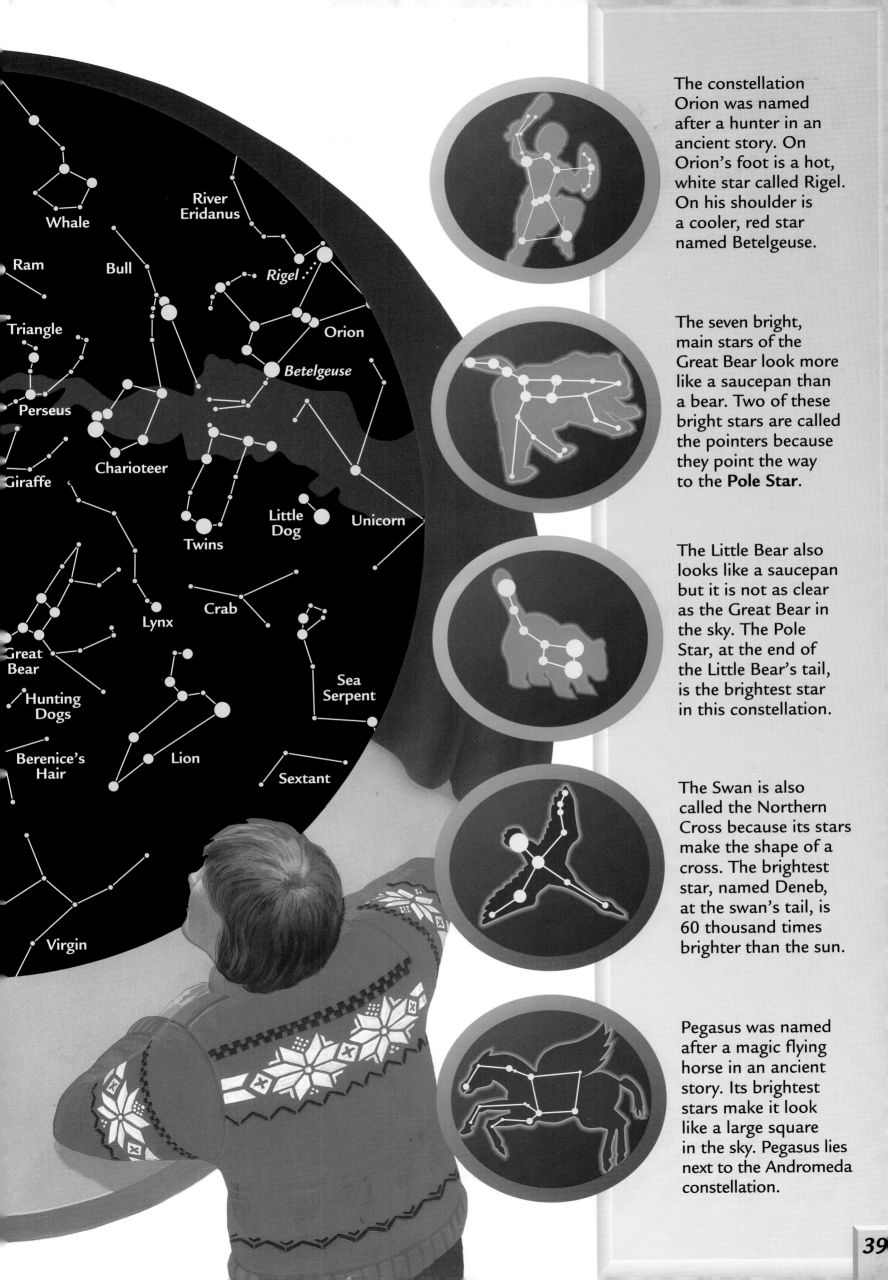

The constellation Orion was named after a hunter in an ancient story. On Orion's foot is a hot, white star called Rigel. On his shoulder is a cooler, red star named Betelgeuse.

The seven bright, main stars of the Great Bear look more like a saucepan than a bear. Two of these bright stars are called the pointers because they point the way to the **Pole Star**.

The Little Bear also looks like a saucepan but it is not as clear as the Great Bear in the sky. The Pole Star, at the end of the Little Bear's tail, is the brightest star in this constellation.

The Swan is also called the Northern Cross because its stars make the shape of a cross. The brightest star, named Deneb, at the swan's tail, is 60 thousand times brighter than the sun.

Pegasus was named after a magic flying horse in an ancient story. Its brightest stars make it look like a large square in the sky. Pegasus lies next to the Andromeda constellation.

Whale
River Eridanus
Ram
Bull
Rigel
Triangle
Orion
Betelgeuse
Perseus
Giraffe
Charioteer
Little Dog
Unicorn
Twins
Lynx
Crab
Great Bear
Hunting Dogs
Sea Serpent
Berenice's Hair
Lion
Sextant
Virgin

Constellations
of the southern skies

Many constellations, or groups of stars, were named thousands of years ago. Some, such as the Great Dog or the Whale, were named after an animal. Others, such as the Centaur, took their names from creatures or people in ancient stories. In the past, sailors traveling across the ocean used the constellations to find their way. During these long voyages, some new constellations were discovered. They were given names, such as the Sails, after parts of a ship.

▶ This picture shows the main constellations you can see in the southern half of the world. Such places as Australia and most of South America are in this part of the world.

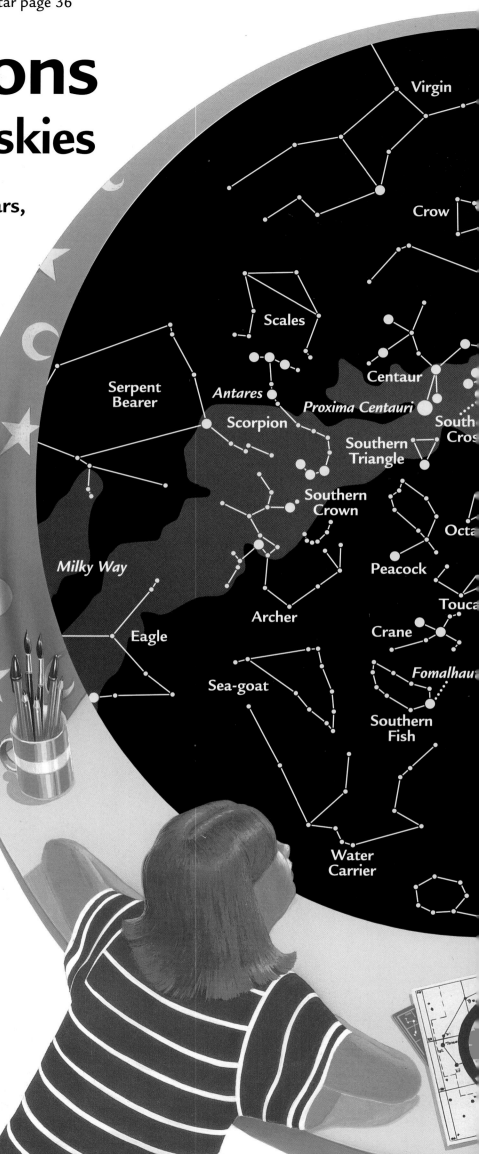

Factfile

Some constellations, such as Orion, can be seen in the southern sky for half of the year and the northern sky for the other half.

The Southern Fish constellation has just one bright star, called Fomalhaut. Long ago, an ancient people thought that Fomalhaut guarded heaven.

The Sea Serpent is the largest constellation in the sky.

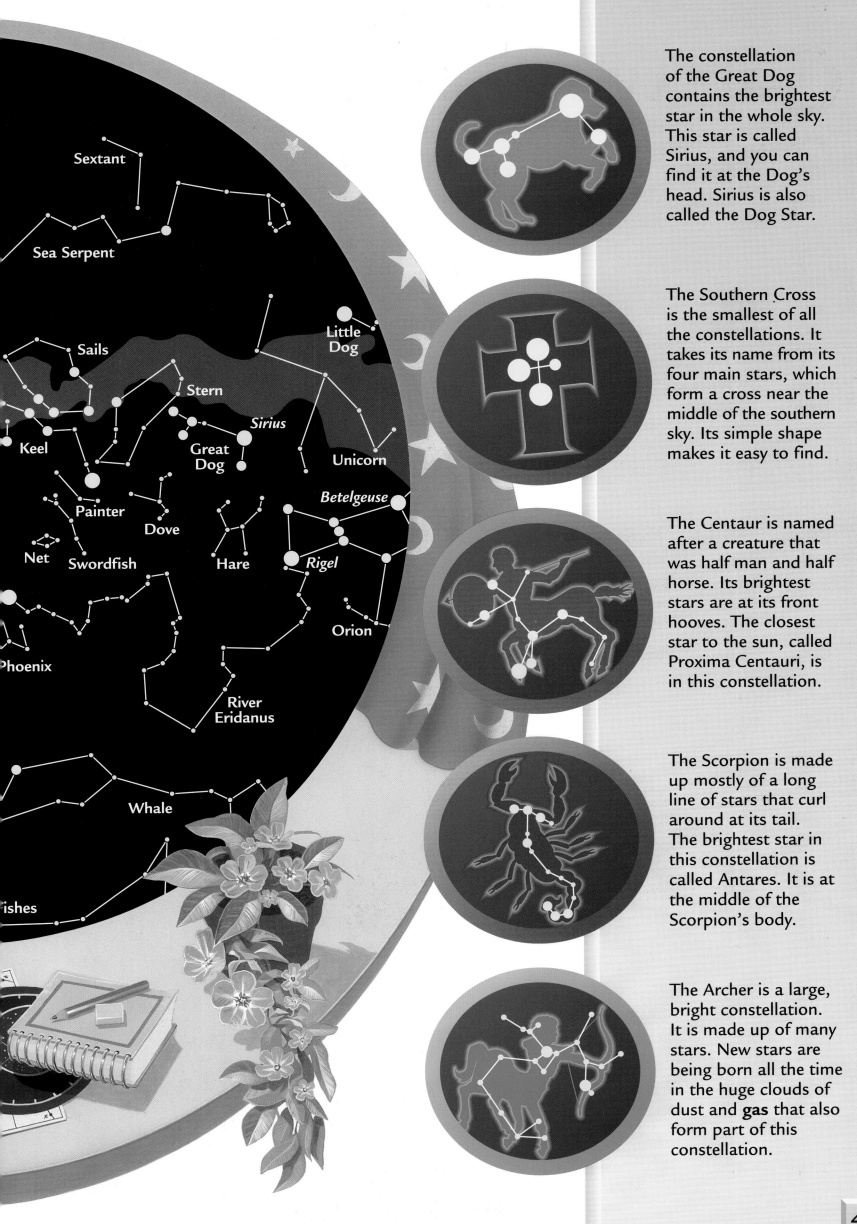

The constellation of the Great Dog contains the brightest star in the whole sky. This star is called Sirius, and you can find it at the Dog's head. Sirius is also called the Dog Star.

The Southern Cross is the smallest of all the constellations. It takes its name from its four main stars, which form a cross near the middle of the southern sky. Its simple shape makes it easy to find.

The Centaur is named after a creature that was half man and half horse. Its brightest stars are at its front hooves. The closest star to the sun, called Proxima Centauri, is in this constellation.

The Scorpion is made up mostly of a long line of stars that curl around at its tail. The brightest star in this constellation is called Antares. It is at the middle of the Scorpion's body.

The Archer is a large, bright constellation. It is made up of many stars. New stars are being born all the time in the huge clouds of dust and **gas** that also form part of this constellation.

Go to Astronomer page 8, Star page 36, Telescope page 10

Galaxy

A galaxy is a huge family of stars, dust and **gas** that is held together by **gravity**. The biggest galaxies contain **billions** of stars. Astronomers have counted millions of galaxies in the **universe** using powerful telescopes, but they think there are still many more to be found. Some galaxies shoot out jets of hot gas from their centers, which travel far into space at high speeds.

Nebula
A cloud of gas and dust inside a galaxy is called a nebula. Some nebulae shine brightly, but others are dark. The Horsehead Nebula, above, is a dark cloud shaped like a horse's head. You can see it only because it shows up against the glowing red clouds behind it.

Milky Way
The sun and the Earth lie inside a galaxy called the Milky Way. It is shaped like a spiral, with a bulge in the middle and long, curved arms containing millions of stars. All these stars are moving around the center of the galaxy. You can see part of the Milky Way from the Earth. It looks like a faint band of light across the sky.

Spiral arm
The spiral arms contain glowing gas clouds where new stars are born.

Sun and Earth
The sun and the Earth lie in one of the spiral arms near the edge of the Milky Way.

Types of galaxies

Galaxies have different shapes. A spiral galaxy has arms curling out from a ball at its center. Some also have a bar across the middle and are called barred spirals. An **elliptical** galaxy has a round or squashed oval shape. Galaxies without any special shape are called irregular.

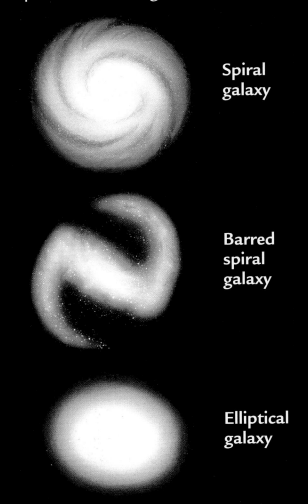

Spiral galaxy

Barred spiral galaxy

Elliptical galaxy

Other galaxies

The billions of galaxies in the universe are not spread evenly through space. They lie together in groups called clusters. Sometimes, a large galaxy in the center of one cluster has swallowed up nearby smaller galaxies. The Andromeda Galaxy in this picture is one of the nearest galaxies to the Milky Way and belongs to the same group. It is also about the same size and shape as the Milky Way. The two bright patches are small elliptical galaxies close to the Andromeda Galaxy.

Expanding universe

Astronomers have discovered that distant galaxies are moving away from the Milky Way and also from each other. This proves that the whole universe is expanding, or becoming bigger. In billions of years, the universe may stop expanding. If it does stop, scientists believe that the universe might squash together.

Farther apart

Here the universe has expanded, so the galaxies are farther apart from each other.

43

Amazing facts

On these pages, you can discover amazing facts about space. You can find out how hot the planets are and how fast they are traveling. You can also learn about the people and animals that have journeyed into space.

How fast are you moving?

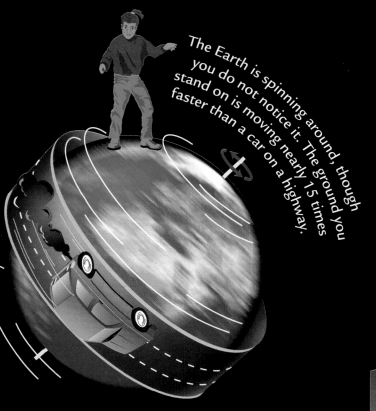

The Earth is spinning around, though you do not notice it. The ground you stand on is moving nearly 15 times faster than a car on a highway.

As the Earth spins, it also races around the sun. It travels over 100 times faster than a jumbo jet, though you don't feel this movement at all.

Which planet is...

The hottest?
On Venus, the **temperature** reaches over 860 °F (460 °C) which is about eight times hotter than the hottest temperature ever recorded on Earth.

The coldest?
Pluto receives little heat from the sun. Its temperature sinks to about -387 °F (-220 °C), which is more than twice as cold as the coldest place on the Earth.

Exploring space

Here are some of the most important dates in the history of space travel.

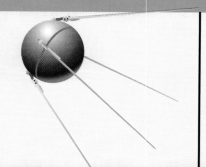

1957

The first satellite, Sputnik 1, was launched by the Soviet Union. This **launch** began the space age.

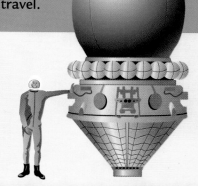

1961

Yuri Gagarin became the first person to fly in space. He circled around the Earth in less than two hours.

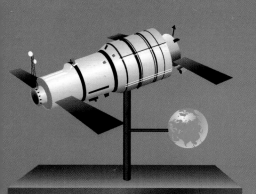

First space station
Salyut 1 was a Soviet space station launched in 1971. A crew of three people lived and worked in it for three weeks while it circled around the Earth.

Longest stay on the moon
In 1972, on the last Apollo trip, Eugene Cernan and Harrison Schmitt spent three days on the moon, exploring its surface in their buggy.

Which animals have traveled into space?

Dog
In 1957, a dog called Laika became the first living thing to travel in space. Laika proved that it was safe for people to travel in space too.

Spider
In 1973, two spiders, called Anita and Arabella, lived in the Skylab space station. They showed that spiders could spin webs in space as well as on Earth.

Jellyfish
In 1991, over 2,000 jellyfish were taken on board the space shuttle to see how well they could swim in space. Scientists discovered that the fish became confused and swam in circles instead of straight ahead.

Different sizes

It is difficult to imagine the sizes of objects in space because they are so enormous. This picture compares the sizes of the sun, moon, Earth, and Jupiter. Imagine the sun is a large beachball...

...then, Jupiter is the size of a tennis ball,...

...the Earth is the size of a pea,...

...and the moon is the size of a pinhead.

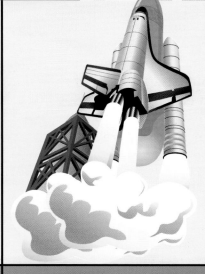

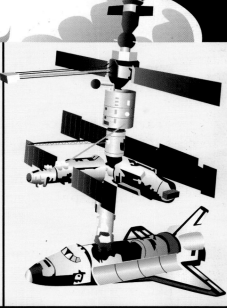

1969
During the Apollo 11 mission, U.S. astronaut Neil Armstrong became the first person to walk on the moon.

1975
The Apollo and Soyuz **spacecrafts** linked up, beginning the first joint U.S.-Soviet space mission.

1981
The space shuttle Columbia made its first flight ever. It stayed in space for over two days.

1995
The space shuttle Atlantis docked with the Mir space station for the first time.

Glossary

atmosphere A layer of **gas** that surrounds a **planet**, star, or **moon**. The Earth's atmosphere, which is called the air, is a mixture of different gases.

billion A number meaning one thousand million, written as 1,000,000,000.

booster rocket A small rocket that is attached to a large space rocket to give extra power at takeoff.

canyon A deep rocky passage with steep sides that lies in between mountains or hills.

core The center of a **planet**, star, or **moon**.

crater A round, shallow hole in the ground that is made when a rock from space hits a **planet** or **moon**.

electricity A form of **energy** that makes **machines**, such as a space telescope, work.

elliptical Almost round like a circle or long and thin like a squashed oval.

energy The force that makes things move or work. Energy can be seen as light or felt as heat.

engine The part of a **machine**, such as a rocket, that burns **fuel** to make it work or move.

false color Color added to a photograph of an object, such as a galaxy, to make it look clearer.

fuel A material that burns in an **engine** and makes it work. Rocket engines burn fuel very fast.

gas A substance, such as air, that has no shape and can only be felt if it moves.

gravity The force that pulls things toward the Earth's surface or toward each other.

laboratory A building or room where scientists work, using special equipment.

lander The part of a **spacecraft** that lands on the surface of a **planet** or **moon**.

launch To lift off from Earth on a journey into space.

launch pad The place where rockets take off.

lunar lander The part of the Apollo **spacecraft** that landed on the moon.

liquid A substance that flows and that has no fixed shape, such as the water of a river.

machine Something with moving parts that does useful work, such as a **spacecraft** that travels to another **planet** or the moon.

moon A natural object in space that travels around a **planet**. A moon is smaller than its planet.

orbit The curved path of an object as it travels in space around a larger object. A **planet** orbits the sun and a satellite orbits the Earth.

oxygen A **gas** in the air that most living things need to breathe to stay alive.

planet A large, round object in space, such as the Earth, that travels around the sun or another star.

Pole Star The name of the star that lies almost directly above the North Pole, which is the most northern place on the Earth.

pollution Unwanted material that spills into the air, sea, or land and damages it.

radio wave An invisible ray that travels through air or space, carrying information that can be made into sounds or pictures.

solid When a material has a firm shape that you can feel.

spacecraft Any **vehicle**, such as a rocket or space probe, that flies in space.

temperature How hot or cold something is.

universe The whole of space and everything in space, including the Earth, stars, and galaxies.

vehicle A **machine**, such as a rocket, that moves people or things from place to place.

volcano An opening in the Earth's surface from which ash or hot rock explodes.

weightless Floating in space and feeling as if you weighed nothing.

Index

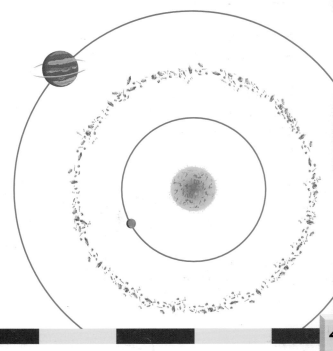